Maldives

Vincenzo Berghella

Copyright Page

Copyright year: 2013

ISBN No:

From the same author: (see also www.lulu.com)

- **Obstetric Evidence Based Guidelines.** Informa Healthcare, London, UK, and New York, USA (2007) [English]

- **Maternal Fetal Evidence Based Guidelines.** Informa Healthcare, London, UK, and New York, USA (2007)[English]

- **Laughter. the best medicine. Jokes for everyone.** (2007) [English]

- **Ridere, la migliore medicina. Barzellette per bambini.** (2007) [Italiano]

- **My favorite quotes.** (2009) [English]

- **In medio stat virtus – Citazioni d'autore.** (2009) [Italiano]

- **Quello che di voi vive in me.** (2009) [Italiano]

- **Dall'altra parte dell'oceano.** (2010) [Italiano]

- **Preterm Birth: Prevention and Management.** Wiley-Blackwell. Oxford, United Kingdom. (2010) [English]

- **From father to son.** (2010) [English]

- **Sollazzi.** (2010) [Italiano]

- **The land of religions.** (2011) [English]

- **Giramondo.** (2011) [Italiano]

- **Obstetric Evidence Based Guidelines.** Informa Healthcare, London, UK, and New York, USA (2012; Second Edition)[English]

- **Maternal Fetal Evidence Based Guidelines.** Informa Healthcare, London, UK, and New York, USA (2012; Second Edition)[English]

- **Trip to London.** (2012) [English]

- **Il primo amore non si scorda mai.** (2012) [Italiano]

- **On the other side of the ocean.** (2013) [English translation of 'Dall'altra parte dell'oceano - 2007]

A splendid trip in paradise

The planning

We had been dreaming about this trip for years. We always knew that in 2013 Paola turned 50, and the plan was to go somewhere exceptional. So for at least the three prior years, my wife Paola, as well as our sons Andrea and Pietro, currently 15 and 13, and me, have been looking up resorts, asking friends, reading guides, and just imagining what would be a spectacular, unforgettable place to visit.

Planning is one of the best parts of any journey. For a long time, Paola's desire was to go to Bora Bora, in Polynesia. She kept on showing us these paradisiacal pictures of palafitte (water villas) in all-inclusive resorts, such as Club Med. She kept one of these images in her computer desktop, as well as own mind. Moreover, none of us has ever been to Oceania.

When came time to actually look for a suitable period of time for us all four to take vacation together, the last week of March 2013 revealed itself to be the best one. Andrea and Pietro both had spring-break during that week, and Paola and I had enough back-up at our respective jobs to be able to take a break.

Once the time is set, Paola is indefatigable and meticulous at scanning by internet the best resorts in the world. Her idea is to go somewhere sunny, where we can all spend quality time together and enjoy the beach. She is not that fancy, and knows what she likes.

While the initial dream was Bora Bora, she also begins to compare hundreds of web sites, looking up hotels, shores, type of sand, pools, costs, special offers, flights, weather in the region at the time of our travel, and many other details that can make or break a great trip.

Our Berghella family does a lot of talking, especially at the dinner table, every evening. In 2012, the conversations soon begin to be polarized by discussions on New Zealand, Fiji, the Cook Islands, and other places which all sound very exotic to us. It's pretty clear that Paola, and really all of us, want to make this special, and go somewhere far, warm, with pristine waters to swim in.

Somehow, looking up travel books had convinced us that Fiji, again in Polynesia, may be the best place to go. Paola even bought two travel guides to look up details. But she soon realized that in March it rains a lot in Fiji, and, with amazing honesty, Lonely Planet talked about 'lots of mud' at that time.

So we began to change geographically, now thinking more seriously about Seychelles, Mauritius, Maldives, and other fantastic options. Several mates, including my beloved brother Michele, and close friend Ignazio, had gone to the Maldives, and raved about them.

These were better recommendations any guide can give you. Paola checked out the weather, which was supposed to be in the upper 90's and beautiful. Then, for a couple of months, we began to gauge flights, for a while stuck on a 28-hour option that would take us from Philadelphia to Paris, then to Colombo, in Sri Lanka, and finally to Male, the capital and only airport in the Maldives.

For the place to stay, we had several options, but Ignazio and his wife Rossana had told us they had had a great time in Club Med. As we had gone on several vacations with them, we knew we could trust their judgment, and they knew our desires. Once Paola figured out an even briefer, with only one stop, and cheaper flight plan, we knew we had our place.

It dawned on us that we were indeed going for a dream vacation when we visited our good friends in Rome, Italy, over the Christmas holiday at the end of 2012. I saw my high school friend Marco, who has been wonderful about keeping in touch all these years. He is usually calm and collected, and in fact one of his nicknames, since secondary school times in Italy, has been James Dean.

But this time he was struggling a bit, with a sweet and beautiful but hyperactive four-year old daughter, a busy and unrewarding job, and the usual chaos of living in Rome. So, at some point during our open conversation in the leaving room of other friends of ours, he busted out, "I really need a vacation in the Maldives!" To him, like to many others, spending holidays in these islands is the top of all desires, the cure for all modern life stresses.

Until the final booking, a couple of months before the dates of the trip, we tried to go to the Maldives with my brother Michele and his lovely wife Donatella. But unfortunately we could not come to an agreement, despite coming close.

As usual, Paola starts making luggage preparation a week in advance. But packing is relatively easy this time: masks and snorkels, sunscreen, sun hats, three-pin UK-style adaptors, plenty of books, sunglasses, bathing suits, some t-shirts, Lycra swim shirts (which we'll never use), a lot of sun protection (which we'll use plenty every day), and flip-flops. We do not need much else.

Thursday, March 21

While some in the US think they are the center of the world, it's not that easy to travel out from America to Asia. Luckily, planes now have made the world much smaller. While 99% of the time we travel out of Philadelphia International Airport, this time we drive to New York JFK Airport.

We have booked parking in the Long Term parking lot, which works out easily and smoothly. The check in is routine, simple, like we are going to Chicago or something. Once we check in the luggage, we realize we will not see it for about another 24 hours, when we hope to arrive in the Maldives.

New York-Doha, in Qatar is our first, long flight. It is about10,778 kilometers, or about 6,700 miles. Smartly – and also the cheapest option - we are booked on Qatar Airways, the only 5-star airline in the world. Here are some of its pluses which we noticed.

First, personnel are nice. They treat passengers with outmost courtesy. They smile, are attentive to needs. They offer small candies and towelettes to clean hands even before take-off. The computer and video in front of each seat is the best I've ever seen. The display is almost as big as my laptop screen, 11-inches.

The movie selection is made up of over 100 movies. These include all of the ones currently still in theaters, as well as recent Oscar winners or nominees. So I watch Argo (best movie), Lincoln (best actor), and Life of Pi (best director). An over 12 hour flight goes much faster with such great entertainment.

There are also classic movies, movies from several different countries, and most can be heard in several languages. The movies can also be subtitled, per viewer's choice, in over 14 languages, including Malayalam, Sinhalese, and Tagalog. This is when one realizes that we are surrounded truly by people from all corners of the world, in this case, in particular, from all of Asia.

There are in fact over one thousand different shows to watch on our flight. One can, of course, watch over a hundred different of TV shows, listen to music, and even play video games with a powerful and fancy remote control. Pietro does not miss the chance.

We fly right over Pescara, my home town in Italy, and I do think about my parents down below. I'll see them in two months, I cannot wait.

Friday, March 22

We arrive in Doha at about 6pm local time. There is an 8-hour difference in time zones between Qatar and the US. In Qatar, despite the British influence, and the ubiquitous signs both in English and Arabic, the distance is reported in kilometers, not in miles. The electric plugs instead are the large, three-pronged and triangular British ones. We are ready, and have plenty of adaptors for our iPad, iPhone, iPods, and MacBook Pro.

A few minutes even just in Doha's International Airport in this capital of Qatar gives us the strong impression that this is a rich country, quickly moving up in the world (they'll host the 2022 soccer World Cup!), and with tremendous resources, growth, and vitality.

Europe was leader in the 19th century, with Queen Victoria and the British Empire dominating much of the world, but also mighty France with its presence in Africa, the huge Spanish influence in Central and South America, and Brazil and smaller colonies for the sailors of Portugal.

The United States of America were the great dominators of the 20th century. The USA won both of the first two and only World Wars. Globalization of travel and trade, controlled in large part by Americans, had as one of its many consequences the fact that English became the second language of most of the 7 billion people who then saw the start of the next century.

But the 21st century is Asia's to dominate. And its influence can be felt already anywhere in the world. China and India are not only the most populous, but quickly becoming, especially China, the true financial power of the world. A lot of other Asian nations are also booming.

Qatar, for example, is the country with the highest average personal income in the world. It is an astonishing $100,000 (in 2010), which means that half of the people here makes more than this. If one criterion for happiness is earning $80,000 or more, Qataris must be one of the most financially happy people in the world.

The country itself is super-rich. In 2010, the economy grew an amazing 19%, which was the fastest growth of any nation in the world. This wealth is due to production and exports of natural gas, oil, petrochemicals, and related industries.

It's hard to know where the name Qatar comes from. It might come from the Persian word 'Gwadar,' which means 'port.' Qatar is a small peninsula off the much larger peninsula of Saudi Arabia, its only border to the south. The other three sides are all bathed by the Persian Gulf.

On this east coast of the Arabian peninsula, from north to south, there are other sites recently made famous by their wealth and progress, such as Kuwait and closer Bahrain to the north, and then to the south of Qatar, Abu Dhabi and Dubai.

Qatar was a British protectorate until 1971, when it gained independence. Its current (2013) population estimate is about just less than two million. Interestingly, the vast majority of this population has recently moved here, and is not originally from Qatar. The true Qataris are only about 250,000, but there is been tremendous immigration, from all over the world, in particular from other Asian countries.

We notice this in Doha's airport, where the people cover the complete gamut of the Asian facial and cultural traits. We see Koreans, Chinese, Japanese, Malaysians, Filipinos, but also Saudis, Nepalese, Bahrain, Indians, Pakistani, Kurds, Sikhs, and many whose facial traits, at time darker at times lighter, we cannot guess with accuracy.

Clearly the world is vast. But my strong impression is that it is made up of wonderful people, and the only reason some may hate each other is because we do not know each other. Religion is certainly one of the biggest dividers we have. Seeing a turban on some man's head evokes in us 'westerners' a foreign, strange, and therefore automatically 'fear' feeling. The same occurs when we see a long white robe and veil worn by some Arabic men. I imagine they must have the same impression looking at our jeans, or our skirts.

Each of us should have close friends of each of the other main religions. The fact I went out for almost two years with Betsy made me greatly understand, appreciate, and admire the Jewish faith. Daoud, my close Algerian friend, prays five times a day, and is one of the gentlest and most polite person I've ever met; he is generous, friendly, indefatigable. He'll certainly make paradise, and is one to admire while on earth.

Several of people I spend most of my day with, are MFM fellows, and these have been Hindu, Buddhist, and of several other religions. I have openly remarked in several occasions that at times each of us at the dinner table have been of a different religious affiliation. But indeed, we all work harmoniously with the same goals, in the same office, for the same organizations.

It's only my third time in Asia. Before, I've been to South-East Asia, in particular Thailand, Malaysia, and Cambodia, and that opened up my mind to this amazing continent. Two years ago we were in Israel, a state, in itself, unique. But this current journey is making me see more of the Islamic Middle East, as both Qatar and the Maldives are 100% Muslim, and a mix of most of the different Asian cultures and nationalities. The Maldives is 100% Sunni Muslim. These are worlds which I had not directly come across before, and studied only minimally, certainly not enough and almost not at all, in my life so far.

Qatar extends on an area of about 11,571 km², which makes it the 164th state for size, so, one of the smallest. One the other hand in terms of happiness, Qatar is a monarchy. It has been ruled as an absolute and hereditary emirate by the Al Thani family since the mid-19th century. Back then, it was poor, and known mostly for its pearl hunting.

There is a varied and colorful humanity at Doha's airport. Shopping is king, with the usual Givenchy, Dior, Ferrero, Mercedes, Maserati, and other global brands dominating, and only may be less than 5% of the merchandise being clearly original from Qatar.

There is a mosque, smoking rooms, lounge rooms, VIP rooms, and all and more of the modern amenities of a large international airport. Andrea and Pietro get two mango shakes and a couple of protein bars. Andrea and I cannot get in the VIP lounges, somehow being a gold member of Star Alliance is not enough.

While waiting, Andrea and I go through the pages of the book '1,000 places before you die.' We review each site and enter our initials

(VB for me, AB for Andrea, PB for Pietro, and PL for Paola) to the ones we have been to. We get through the whole book, we still have not counted up the numbers, and we still have plenty of wonderful places to visit.

We board the flight from Doha, Qatar, to Male, Maldives, at around 1am (Saturday time). From New York to Doha, Qatar, I probably slept about four or five hours. I manage to sleep a couple of more hours in the about five-hour flight from Doha to Male.

Between 5 and 6 am, the sun rises, and some people begin to peak at the sunrise on the Indian Ocean. Paola and Andrea peak from the window and begin to voice many 'uh's' and 'ah's' at the marvelous spread of atolls below.

Saturday, March 23

We land on time, at around 7:30am. The baggage arrives quickly. We take a boat ride to get to the island where Club Med is. It takes about half an hour, traversing limpid waters, from Male, to Kani, which is the island where we are directed.

Why did the Maldives form right here, in this particular part of the globe? The Maldives are the result of the pushing against each other of two tectonic plates. Basically, the tectonic plate on which India sits, keeps on abutting in a northwest direction against the tectonic plate of the Arabian Peninsula. So over the millennia underwater volcanoes formed on the bottom of the south-west Indian Ocean, that here is over 2,000 meters in depth (about 6,600 feet).

These volcanoes then formed oceanic mountains, a long series of underwater peaks vertically placed on the map on the west side of southern part of the Indian Ocean. The long mountain ridge emerged from the water edge, but was soon overcome by water and wind erosion. The Maldivian atolls sit on top of a 2,000km-long volcanic ridge of basalt that was formed over 50 million years ago.

The Maldives were created when corals populated these underwater mountain tops, and made them emerge near water top level. Coral polyps are tiny, tentacle creatures that feed on plankton. These coral polyps are invertebrates, and have sac-like bodies and calcareous skeletons. The extract calcium from the water around them, and use this to excrete tiny, cup-shaped, limestone skeletons.

A coral reef is the rock-like accumulation of millions of these polyp skeletons. As polyps die, new polyps attach themselves to the skeleton under them, in successive layers. So only the outer layer of coral is alive. The slow accumulation of dead corals can make, over the course of millennia, mountains. In fact, in the Maldives this growth, one of the fastest in the world, has been calculated. It is about 1.25cm (half an inch) per year. That means coral rock mountains grow 125 meters (410 feet) in only 10,000 years: that is fast in geological terms!

So, on top of the volcanic ridge of basalt, in the waters under the Maldives, there is a plateau of accumulated coral stone over 2,000-meter thick. By my calculations, these took just 160,000 years to make. This coral stone mantle comes to about 300 to 500 meters below the oceanic surface. But coral grow best in shallow, clear water, and especially when waves and currents for the open sea bring plenty of oxygen and nutrients. Live coral wants to be close to the water surface.

Changes in sea levels, and in the level of the underlying plateau, further characterize the coming to be of the atolls. When the sea level rises, the coral grows upwards to stay near the sea surface, as originally described by Darwin in his observations of Pacific atolls. When the water level came down, or the plateau below rose, the top corals would be exposed to weather, die, be eroded, and later, when sank again, form the flat base for new live coral formation, in a never-ending (so far!) process.

The atolls of these paradisiacal islands sit on top of these layers. An atoll is a ring-shaped coral reef including a coral rim that encircles a lagoon partially or completely. There may be coral islands or cays on the coral rim. An atoll can be described as annular reefs enclosing - like a ring-shaped ribbon - a lagoon, with no promontories other than reefs and islets composed of reef detritus. Each atoll is so surrounded by the barrier reef, usually in an oval circle about twice longer in its vertical compared to its horizontal axis.

The barrier reef, made by high deposits of corals accumulated through millennia, is basically a natural defense against the open ocean waters. So inside each of these atolls, the water is calm, with no waves, placid. Somewhat in the middle of these long areas, circumferentially protected by the reef, raise, so to speak, the islands. These islands, circled by the reef, form from accumulated rubble from broken coral in the center of the lagoon. Sand and debris accumulate on these corals, creating sandbars on which eventually vegetation can eventually grow.

The word atoll comes from the Dhivehi (an Indo-Aryan language spoken on the Maldives Islands) word 'atholhu.' Its first recorded use in English was in 1625 as 'atollon' – Charles Darwin recognized its indigenous origin and coined, in his 'The Structure and Distribution of

Coral Reefs,' the definition of atolls as "circular groups of coral islets," that is synonymous with "lagoon-island."

There are about 1,193 islands each surrounded by reef in the Maldives. This number varies a bit, as small islands are born and disappear daily. Later, while at Kani, we saw sandbars rise from the sea at low tide inside our atoll. During diving trips, we would see reef rock emerge from the sea. One can only imagine how treacherous it must be to boat around these atolls without knowing exactly the depth beneath you.

These islands can also be grouped in 26 separate bunches of atolls, that is clusters of hundreds of atolls which themselves form the shape of a big oval. Making it a bit confusing, these large groups of atolls are themselves called 'atolls.' For example, the island where the capital, Male, is, as well as the island were Club Med is, are both in the 'North atoll.'

The highest point on all of the Maldives is only 2.4 meters (about 7'8" feet high).These islands are famous for being one the places on earth most at risk for disappearing if sea levels rise, as a consequence of global warming causing glaciers to melt at the poles.

The area over which the over 1,000 Maldivian islands spread is about 90,000 square kilometers, but the area above water is only 298 sq km, so that the percentage of the country which is water is 99.9%. The city of Austin, in Texas, has a similar land area. The population of the Maldives is about 330,000, of which more than 100,000 live in Male. A million people a year visit them. Maldivians have participated in the Summer Olympics since 1988, but never won a medal, and never participated in the winter Olympics (surprised?).

The Maldivians were converted to Islam in 1,153 CE by Abul Barakat Yoosuf Al Barbary, a North African. Early converts were the sultan and his royal family, and then they sent missionaries to the other islands. Officially, even now in 2013, only Muslims may become citizens of the Maldives, so 100% of Maldivians are Muslims. Interestingly enough, in Club Med, despite more than 50% of the staff was Maldivian, I never saw them pray, or talk, of give any signs of their religion.

In 1573, the Portuguese were forced out of the Maldives by an attack led by Mohammed Thakurufaanu, who so became the first sultan of the third dynasty of the Kingdom of the Maldives. He is the national hero, a kind of George Washington of the Maldives, and the day of his victory is celebrated as National Day.

In 1796, the British declare the Maldives a British Protected Area. Maldivian sultans, nonetheless, continue to rule. The country gains full independence from the UK in 1965, and joins the Commonwealth in 1982. In 1968, the Maldives abolish for good the sultanate, and elect the first president of their new republic, Ibrahim Nasir. The first holiday resort in the Maldives opens in 1972.

In 1998, the El Nino weather system causes water temperatures to rise above 32°C for two weeks. Coral algae die, and the corals in most of the Maldives (except the very southern atolls) lose the colors. This is known as 'coral bleaching.' In 2004, the Indian Ocean tsunami causes inundation and much destruction in the Maldivian atolls. In 2008, the first democratic elections bring Muhammed Nasheed to the presidency. Taxes were introduced for the first time in 2012.

India is currently the Maldives' biggest internationally ally. The Maldivians speak a language unique to these islands. They told me it is a mix of Arabic and Tamil, and has its own alphabet, which to me looks incomprehensible, but most similar to Arabic symbols.

We begin to experience the island we are on, Kani. We have 'landed' on the west side. There is an 80-meter wooden pontoon, or pier, or also called here 'jetty,' that goes to land. The whole island is encircled by bright, white sand. Seen closer now under our feet, this is made of broken up corals. Walking barefoot, as we'll do during most of our stay, one can feel these tiny needles under their feet.

This island, rented exclusively by Club Med, is 800 meters long going approximately west-south-west to east-north-east, and 200 meters wide. There are no cars, no traffic, no noise of any motor. There are actually no motor roads.

The reception is just about 20-30 yards inland from the end of the jetty. We are greeted by Jerry, the only American GO (Gentil Organisateur) in the island, and a couple of Maldivian GOs. As you know by now, every company in the Maldives has, by law, to employ at least 50 percent or more of its workers from Maldivian citizens. They offer us not only lots of info, but also a nice, refreshing ice tea.

Our rooms are large, comfortable, and communicating. Paola loves to have Andrea and Pietro's room right next to ours, so to share space for common goods and luggage, and be able to be with them, and helpful to them, as much as possible. Often we mix up and sleep let's say me and Andrea in one room and Pietro and Paola in another. But this trip, Andrea and Pietro are quite happy to be together in their comfortable, white king bed.

Of course, this arrangement allows for no marital intimacy, but has a lot of advantages. First and foremost, it facilitates a true feeling of one happy, close family. Being together 24/7 for 10 days is, unconsciously, one of the best parts of our trip.

Our rooms, number 19 and 20, are close to the center of the village's life. Through large floor to ceiling sliding windows, open to a ground floor patio, we can see the beach, only about 20 yards away. The busiest bar is only about 30 yards away, on the right, close to the beach, and almost attached to the large, infinity pool. As we wake up early every day, we are always able to reserve two of the long beach chairs, under the palms at the corner of the pool, and strategically the two closest to the bars and the free drinks.

Our next stop is culinary. We the Berghella never miss a meal. And in this all-inclusive resort, the meals are 'free,' and all-you-can-eat. As my will power for free food is next to zero, I end up gaining in eight days on the island at least about an extra pound a day.

While Paola opens up the luggage and organizes all we brought, Pietro Andrea and I dive in the pool, and begin to unwind and relax. From the north-west edge of the poll, one can place its elbows on the low rim, and watch the fantastic view of coral white sand, tall palm trees, and crystalline waters all the way to the horizon.

After lunch we together walk and explore the whole island. I often wear no shoes, except for going to the restaurant for meals, when I use Pietro's extra pair of flip-flops. The south-east shores have even shallower waters, only about a foot and a half deep for about 50 yards out. There are plenty of fish in the waters, and they can be seen clearly as the water seems clearer than a bathtub. Even yellow and red corals are easily seen just with the naked eye, standing.

On this side of the island, there is also another small islet, about 50 by 50 yards, with sand all around, and trees and bushes as its only inhabitants. Andrea and I swim to it, as it is only about 40 yards from our shore.

We also discover a huge soccer field, big enough for at least a 9-on-9 game, with great grass, and full-size goals. Andrea, Pietro, and I play a bit with the four old and beaten up soccer balls just lying there. We also find a basketball court, and two volleyball courts.

Andrea and I later book the dives for the rest of the week. A friendly guy from the Mauritius Islands, called James, helps us. He is blond, blue-eyes, and muscular. I wonder how he ended being from such a fascinating place.

Another fun initial endeavor in any Club Med is figuring out all the free activities. Breakfast is from about 7am until 10am. The GOs tell us later that 7am is 'Tiananmen Square' time, as it is the favorite time for Asian to eat. Yoga and gym activities are usually around 9am, and 2pm.

Snorkeling in big groups by boat off the island is at 10am and 2pm. Late morning there is often also some other activity, such as ping pong (table tennis). From about 10am-12noon, and again 2pm-5pm, one can also take to the lagoon kayaks, and catamarans. There are free sailing lessons every morning.

There are also beach soccer and beach volleyball courts on the white coral shore, as well as badminton and bocce courts. Inside the island, amid the tropical flowers, palms and lush vegetation, there are also a large green-grass full soccer field, and beaten-up basketball court, and a pair of volleyball courts.

For the less sport inclined, there are lounge chairs, and reclining beach chairs everywhere along the shore. Some are under beautiful canopies, or paradisiacal gazebos, usually orange. There are two beach bars, one near the infinity pool, near our rooms, and on the north-west side of the atoll, and one, the Iru bar, on the south-east side of the island, near the second restaurant.

In the evening, we feel so tired that we go to sleep around 8pm local time. There is 9 hour time difference between Philadelphia and the Maldives. We are definitively jet-lagged. Except for the last day, our time to fall asleep in Kani will vary little, and will usually be between 8 and 9pm, very early. We miss all Club Med shows, except for the last one, on Friday.

Sunday, March 24

Each morning while in Kani, I wake up between 5:30 and 6am, given the jet lag. One could take this as a drag, as one of the objectives of a vacation is catching up on sleep. But I probably do not have to catch up much on my sleep, since I try to get about seven and a half to eight hour sleep every night even during the workweek.

But I'm famous for my optimistic outlook, and trying to convert everything to a positive emotion. So, instead of getting mad at waking up so early, I rejoice at the possibilities this brings. First and foremost, I get to see the sunrise every morning, since it occurs just after 6am. Second, I get to gather my thoughts in silence, and meditate, while watching the great spectacle of dawn over the placid Indian Ocean, and I even have some private time to check emails and read the news of the day.

I've now fully embraced the notion that checking email only once a day at most while on vacation has several benefits. First and foremost, I do it so I do not have over 500 emails to go through when I get back after a week off. Secondly, I look at issues much more nonchalantly, and so nothing appears worrisome or urgent while sitting with only a bathing suit on a comfortable padded armchair and feet up on another, while on the edge of the shallow atoll lagoon, watching intermittently baby black-tip sharks go by while the crystal clear waters become ever more sparkling with the rise of the sun.

Thirdly, most my close colleagues do know I'm off, and the few emails I do answer, probably only about a couple a day, make me feel like I still am in 'the mix,' still able to participate and show interest. So checking email is indeed quite a rewarding activity, probably much more here in the Maldives that back in the US.

The Wi-Fi reception at the Iru Bar, on the south-east side of the island, is good enough that I can also scroll down the BBC World news with my iPhone. So I can check if Italy has finally formed a new government after the February elections (unfortunately not!), or which pompous Vatican tradition the new nice and friendly Pope has given up each day.

In the morning, Andrea and I are booked for the Orientation Dive. We go to the jetty, which is the end of the beautiful wooden pier where one arrives or leaves this paradise of Club Med Kani. The instructor is Abel. He is very nice, from Barcelona, but one would never guess is, as he speaks perfect French with his diving pals. His Italian and English are fluent, as well, with the slightest, almost no, accent.

Andrea is a novel scuba diver, fresh from getting his certificate two years ago in the Club Med at Cancun, in Mexico. He actually dove there, while learning, first in the pool, then in calm and clear inland fresh water lagoons, and last in the open waters of Playa del Carmen, near Cozumel.

I began to do scuba diving in 1996, when I got my open water certificate in Hawaii, specifically in Maui, in a super-fast course. Since then, I did scuba dives in several places in the Caribbean, Europe, Thailand, and last in Mexico, with Andrea.

Andrea and I familiarize ourselves with the equipment again. The BCD (Buoyancy Compensation Device) is the 4-lineapparatus that brings air from the oxygen tank to our mouths, and the wetsuit. There are two lines which each go to a separate regulator. The black regulator is the main one, which we wear in our mouths to breath. The yellow one, coming off the yellow line, is for emergencies, and serves to be able to help someone else in need. So that two people can breathe from the same tank in case a buddy runs out of air.

The wetsuit, even if I have an x-large, is nice and tight, and Andrea needs to help zip me up in the back. I am giving five weights (about 2 kilograms each) for buoyancy. Andrea is given three, but we'll discover later in the water that he needs only two, as he is very light. My fins are size 46-47 (about size 12), and Andrea size 45-46 (about size 11.5). The masks are comfortable, with a padded strap in the back.

Abel takes about 15 minutes to explain, while still on the jetty, what we are going to do in the water just off the pier. The only 'students' are Luca – 14 years old -, Stefano – his French-Italian dad -, Andrea, and me. Abel explains we'll do three main exercises under water. Paola and Pietro are looking on, and inside I wish they'll get interested enough that they would want to dive later; but my hopes are in vain.

The first exercise is taking the mask off our faces while under water, and putting it back on. To ensure that one can see again, one must hold the top of the mask, and exhale in the mask with her nose to put back in it some air, to allow visibility.

The second exercise is removing the regulator, letting it go off the hand and float freely, and then finding it again with a particular movement of the right arm. One has to put the straightened right arm on her right thigh, then bend the arm at the elbow and have the right hand touch one's back while moving cephalad, until the tube with the regulator at its end is felt, usually by the right forearm. One then is supposed to put the regulator back in the mouth, and blow hard to release any water, before taking again the first new breath in. This seems fairly easy and straightforward.

The third and last exercise is to mimic a situation in which you have run out of air (the 21% oxygen in the tank). The signal to your buddy, or in this case the dive master, is to move the right open hand horizontally across your neck back and forth, communicating under water the lack of air. One then has to take the extra, yellow regulator from the buddy, remove its own regulator from his mouth, and start instead breathing through the buddy's extra regulator and tank. To avoid getting separated by the current, one should hold each other left forearms, to stay locked in place.

Andrea recalls the instructions for how we jump in the water, once fully geared. One must hold with the right hand the mask and the regulator - already in the mouth - against the face, while the left hand grabs the weight belt at the waist. One dives in the water feet first, by opening the legs just like taking a big step, so not to go down too quickly. Abel in fact warns us that the sandy bottom is close, as the water here is only less than 5-6 feet deep, and so we could hit the bottom hard if we go in with closed parallel legs.

The water here at the end of the jetty is fairly cloudy, with limited visibility. The good thing is, visibility will be perfect in all of our future open water dives. Then Abel makes us do the three exercises he had explained to us so carefully on land. We pass with flying colors.

At 1:45 in the afternoon, we go for the first real open water scuba dive. The dive master is Otto, a Maldivian, who is super-nice. He, just like all Maldivians, is a bit short, perhaps about 5'2", very thin (I guess 100 pounds at most), but shaped like a warrior, with the waistline of a ballerina and the shoulders of a water polo player.

Apart from all the equipment we used the day before, we are given what they call a 'computer,' meaning a special wristwatch. This will tell us in real time the depth and time of the dive, to avoid going deeper than 20 meters (almost 70 feet) and staying longer than about 45 minutes. It also calculates time between dives. This should be at least one hour, to give the body the time to readjust.

We go to the dive site called Aquarium. It will be perhaps our best dive. We stay down about 49 minutes, at a maximum depth of about 20 meters. We see green turtles, and several sharks, both white-tip and black tip ones. The white-tip shark is a non-aggressive, territorial shark, and is about 1.5 meters long, or about 5 feet. Maldivian sharks do not pose any dangers to humans, as they just have too much to eat already. Reef sharks feed on small fish. In 2009, the Maldivian government was the first in the world to outlaw the hunting of sharks, so these waters are really shark sanctuaries.

We also spot during the dive two Napoleon fish, also called Napoleon wrasse and humphead wrasse, which are the largest of these species. These are some of the bigger fish seen in the Maldives, and the ones we see are about 3-4 feet long, quite impressive, as they are also not slim. There are dark green, with a fine vertical pattern. The characteristic hump on the head of the Napoleon becomes larger and more pronounced as the fish ages.

We also see in our dives tons of other different types of fish. Among them, long nose and also collared butterfly fish, masked banner fish with large yellow and black vertical striped, emperor angle fish, and orange fairy basslet. Oriental sweet lips have horizontal (unusual pattern) black and yellow stripes, and black pock-a-dot on yellow background fins and front, with a hint of blue also in the body, and are a remarkable site, especially when seen in shoals of 20 or 30 together.

There are also blue-uned, and convict surgeon fish. Some 'ugly' fish, as they have lots of irregularities in their bodies, are rock cod fish, such as the blue barred or peacock rock cods. Of course, for dozens of other different fish we see I'm not 100% sure of the name.

One of the most striking, and rare sights during this dive, is dolphins. It is Andrea who is the first to spot them. They are at least ten or so, and they are swimming fast about 15 meters below the ocean surface. We quickly spread the news to the Otto and the other divers. Otto will say later that in twelve years of almost daily diving, he has had such sighting occur to him less than the fingers of his hand. Andrea is thrilled.

It's so wonderful to have Andrea as my buddy. I'm very lucky that he has bravely agreed to share the passion for seeing the wonderful world that lives underwater.

There are so many different types of fish in these waters, and they are so beautiful, that it is hard to keep count, and to believe your eyes. A couple of times I catch myself thinking that this must be impossible, as everywhere I look there is a more colorful fish. One could not even dream of a more stunning show.

At a corner in the coral reef, there is enough current that is best for us to grab a rock, and hold on to watch the splendid marine life around us. Dozens of different types of fish go by. It is almost unbelievable, unless one is there to witness it, to see how many different kinds go by. Whoever is responsible for this, is a master, and has done a super-human job.

The Maldives' waters are clear, with excellent visibility. The marine life is rich and not-harmful. In fact, the last shark attack was in 1976. Otto, our dive master, tells us that basically shark attacks are not real; to him, they are something made up by movie writers.

Reefs are often referred to as the rainforests of the sea. This is because they are home to about a quarter of all underwater species, even if they take up only about 0.1% of the ocean's surface. Diving into these waters proves that there are hundreds of different kinds of fish. I dove in the Mediterranean, and there are very few fish there. The Caribbean, the Yucatan peninsula in Mexico, and especially Hawaii, have waters where there is a wonderful sea life, but the one we saw in the Maldives is hard to beat.

In the Maldives, there are about 700 species of fish that live off the reef. Reef fish live inside the atoll lagoons, on and around coral-reef structures. Pelagics instead live in the open sea, but come close to the reef for food. Pelagics include the larger animals, such as turtles, whales, and dolphins.

Elated, on the way out from the jetty at the end of the dive, we confirm we'll scuba again tomorrow morning for two dives in the same excursion.

Lunch is even more delightful after such a morning. The choice of food is vast. There are a lot of fish, but also meat, pasta, pizza, French pastries and desserts, tropical fruits, and several other options, sometimes new to us. Given the clientele in this particular Club Med, there are also wonderful dedicated and long Chinese and Japanese food counters.

At the entrance of the restaurant, on the right, there is always a special treat, often raw fish, Japanese, tuna tartare, Maldivian tuna, etc. In this area there are also fresh juices, such as watermelon, mango, pineapple, and mixed tropical fruit.

Paola, Andrea and Pietro's first aim, once in the restaurant, is finding a table. We often seat closest to the beach, with no roof on our heads, unless it's just too sunny. We quickly befriend the head cook, who is Italian! Alessandro comes from Milan. He is a riot, funny, always smiling. He makes us feel every time like he has invited us to a special meal.

We again overeat. It's impossible to resist trying Alessandro's pastas and pizzas. Then Paola and I, but also Andrea and Pietro, experiment with the spicy Indian, Chinese, or Japanese special treats, usually about ten for each of these different cuisines. Andrea and I also have plenty of fish. Paola and I try several of the many different salads. Pietro, and at times Andrea, cannot resist hamburgers, hot dogs, fries, and the likes.

The desserts are usually about seven or eight different ones, and each of us four routinely gets a sample of each. We then compare which ones we like the most, and at times go for more. There is also a special stand just for ice cream, including vanilla, chocolate, stracciatella, mango, strawberry, and mint chocolate. The waiter manning this stand is an Indian who looks a bit scary, always frowned, but we attach his stand lunch and dinner anyway. On top of the two scoops he serves us, we pour melted chocolate syrup, nuts, and other delicacies.

Through Alessandro the cook, we also later meet Anna, one of the receptionists. She is also from Lombardia, near Milan. She has gentle green eyes, has a foreign language PhD, and speaks seven languages. She is also very helpful and friendly with us, and this comes out naturally. It is clear these GOs are not pretending to be nice because of their jobs on the island. Whoever selects them is doing a great job.

We spend the rest of the day playing sports, rooming around the island, and drinking novel tropical non-alcoholic punches at the two bars. At the pool bar, often it's Iza, a beautiful tall and smiley black girl from Cape Verde, off the west coast of Africa, who serves us. At the Iru bar, on the south-east side of the island, we meet Bartolomeo.

He is the third and last Italian GO, and comes instead from near Benevento, close to Naples. He is one of the barmen. Alessandro and Anna had already voiced their discontent with Italy, and the fact that they were planning a life outside of our nonetheless beloved booth.

Bartolomeo is even bitterer. He had a restaurant/bar in his hometown, on which he and his parents had invested several hundreds of thousands of dollars. Due to the economy, he had to sell it, at much lower than his investment. He was turning 40 in 2013, and was fully aware he could not remain a GO forever. He knew there was no future for him in Italy, and was looking to come perhaps to North America. On the last day, we exchanged emails, and he has since sent me his CV.

On this side of the island, even in the very shallow waters, at all times, in the early morning, during the day, and even after dark, we always see juvenile sharks swimming calmly in the foot-deep water near the shore, inside the lagoon. They are about only a foot and a half long, but they look just like a real fully-formed shark, with their tips just above the water level, but their whole bodies very well visible given the crystal clear water visibility. Paola, Andrea, Pietro and I seem to never tire of watching them swim peacefully.

Monday, March 25

Breakfast here at Club Med is a major meal. There are seeming a hundred choices, hot and cold, familiar and exotic. I try to restrain myself, and usually fill a large bowl with two different types of cereals, red papaya, and peaches in syrup. But it is hard to resist different kinds of French buttery croissants, omelets, juices, and other treats.

Andrea and I have a8:20am appointment at the top of the pier (jetty) for our 2nd and 3rd open water dives. Today a beautiful girl from French-speaking Martinique, Lola, is our dive master. She is probably the most low key, and smiley, of the instructors. The first dive is at a site called Maagiri. Andrea and I go down at a maximum depth of almost 21 meters, and stay down for a total of about 40 minutes.

I practically run out of air, and must surface about five minutes before the others. Lola feels bad for me, but I had signaled to her first when I was at 50 bars of oxygen (with a closed fist), and later even that I had run out of air (by passing my open hand horizontally under my chin back and forth). But she, so she claimed, did not see these signs, as she had the sun in her face while looking up at me. So I did not even have time to equalize at five meters, as one should for at least three minutes. Andrea was a bit scared, he told me later, not to see me next to him for those few minutes.

Today, a French diver called Vincent also comes with us and takes beautiful underwater photos, which I'll end up paying lots of money for. But they are remarkable memories, especially the ones of me and Andrea underwater together.

The second dive is at Himmafushi. Both Andrea and I go even deeper at past 22 meters, and I manage to stay down for 42 minutes without running out of air, but with only about 20-30 bars of pressed oxygen left.

We spot again many fish. Anemone fish are among my favorites. They are about 11cm long (4-5 inches), bright orange except for a large white stripe around their neck area. We spot also Anemone fish of different, but often just as bright, colors. They get their names for the fact that they live among the venomous tips of sea anemone tentacles, to hide from predators. The mucous coating protects them from the poison. It's wonderful to see them move among the soft tentacles, which wave more beautifully than a wheat field touched by a spring breeze.

There are fourteen different species of angelfish in the Maldives. The three-spot one is bright yellow, with impressive, puffy, blue lips. It's also about 5 or 6 inches long, usually. Regal, also called empress, angelfish have bright yellow bodies with vertical dark blue and white stripes. But perhaps my absolute favorite is the empress angelfish with orange and blue vertical lines. It is just so well designed and joyfully bright, with my two favorite colors. Instead, the larger emperor, or imperial, angelfish have horizontal blue and yellow lines, with a dark blue mask and gill markings.

Hidden inside a coral reef, we see two moray eels. We'll see them practically in every dive, and even around the lagoon in Club Med, close to shore in shallow waters. Usually, they can be seen just poking their head out of holes in the reef edge. If one is patient and waits long enough, they often come out, and, as gentle agile serpents they move swiftly through the bottom of the sea. One is tempted to poke a finger at their open mouths: but be careful, as they have a strong bite, and they do not let go. One French guest diver shows later on the boat a Band-Aid covering such a bite from a couple of days prior.

Near these eels, we spot a lionfish. These are remarkable fish, with long, soft, thin, almost transparent, and at the same times brightly colored (shades of red, usually) fanlike fins. They can deliver a nasty sting. These fins are used to trap prey. This remarkable shape, ever changing, makes them experts at camouflage.

We see many different kinds of butterfly fish. They are about 5 to 12 inches long, with a flattened body. Some – such as Bennet's butterfly fish - have a 'false eye' near the tail to make predators think it's a larger fish facing the other way. My favorite kind is probably the black pyramid butterfly fish, with its large bands of white and black stripes. But we see also pacoon, black backed, raccoon, Madagascar, tread fin, saddle back, and other remarkable, always colorful, often funny-shaped butterfly fish.

A bunch of eagle rays, closely related to the larger manta rays, 'flies by', in their characteristically calm, large, slow-motion ways. They are some of the most remarkable sights in these waters, as they are so much different than any other fish. They are similar to US B-2 Stealth bombers.

At times, one spots bigger fish than most, as in general most reef fish are about between 5 and 10 inches long. Parrotfish is bigger, usually about 20 inches long, and 'fatter' looking, not as flattened as most of the smaller fish. There are over 20 different species of parrotfish in the Maldives, so everyone seems to be a bit different than the other. With strong, beak-like, usually differently-colored mouths, they scrape and bite the coral surface, then grind up the coral chunks, swallowing and filtering to extract nutrients, in general algae. They sometimes can be seen 'discharging' clouds of coral-like feces.

Another common fish in the trigger fish, of which there are over 12 species in the Maldives. It is also 20 inches, and up to 30 inches, long. Trigger fish are carnivorous. Orange striped trigger fish can even be seen in shallow reef waters, and Toto is such an example. Toto is a large trigger fish who lives along the jetty in Club Med. Andrea, Pietro and Paola regularly stop by, usually once a day, to feed him some bread. He is always there waiting, surrounded by lots of smaller fish ready for the leftover crumbs.

Instead, clown trigger fish has large, round, white blotches on the lower half of its body. These, unlike most other fish, usually swim alone, not in herds. We also see several Picasso trigger fish, which are remarkable because they pack at least 5 or 6 different bright colors on the 6-8 inch bodies, such as orange, blue, yellow, black, green, and others, usually in precise strokes of paint in each different parts of their figure. There are also red-toothed, yellow-margin, scythe, and other kinds of trigger fish we spot at different times.

Perhaps one of the most remarkably-finned fish we see is the Moorish idol. It's also about 6 to 8 or so inches long, usually with attractive vertical yellow and black large vertical bands, and has a characteristic long, streamer-like extension to the upper dorsal fin, like a long band gently flying in the water.

We exchange plenty of 'ok' signs underwater, to signal each other, and especially the dive master, that all is well. I often run out of air. We are given 200 bar of compressed air, and at 50 bars the gauge goes into the 'red zone.' Usually the guide then decides to end the dive, which involves going to about 5 meters, and holding there steady for about 3 minutes to decompress. Therefore, one cannot wait until there is much less than this amount of air in the tank, to avoid not being able to do the safety measure of decompressing.

The water is so warm in the Maldives that some divers are not even wearing wetsuits. Indeed, a swim is not even that refreshing. But it is wonderful to never feel cold in this ocean, even at depths of over 20 meters. And even during the later night dive.

During the trips back and forth to the scuba sites, we befriend a few of the other divers. Once, I speak at length with an attractive couple, both probably in their late 20's. He is a Swiss boy leaving in Zurich, and she is Swedish girl who lives in London. They met while both working in Banking in the UK. They speak about 8 languages between the two of them. Many of the other divers are friendly, often laughing, middle-aged French divers.

Pietro and Paola unfortunately do not want to try diving. In fact, they have not even been to any of the organized snorkeling trips. But they state they would go if Andrea and I joined them. So, after another abundant lunch, we all four head to the end of the jetty for group snorkeling.

The 45 minutes of snorkeling are actually quite enjoyable, even if tiring, as we swim the whole time. We see one huge – over 3 feet long - sting ray lying on the plateau. It's great to be having fun together as a family in such a wonderful environment. We are never far from each other. We help the other spot newer, more colorful fish during the whole dive.

On the boat trip back, Andrea begins to feel cold. In fact, a bit later in the evening, he complains he is unwell. He feels warm to touch to both Paola and I. She, uncharacteristically, did not bring a thermometer, so we never find out if he has a fever, but he definitely looks it, with bright red cheeks.

Tuesday, March 26

In the morning, we recount to our dive instructors that we, the day prior, instead of following their advice to rest for at least 2-3 hours after the double scuba dives, went snorkeling. Their diagnosis is clear: we did too much, and Andrea probably had a case of dehydration. In fact, a full night of rest and plenty of fluids begin to improve the situation. Nonetheless, in the infirmary, is temperature was still 37.5^{0}C (99.5^{0}F), even after 400mg of ibuprofen.

Instead, I was still felling ok after the previous day spent mainly in the Maldivian waters diving and snorkeling, and I had booked for myself two other morning scuba dives on Tuesday. These would be my 4th and 5th dives, and I had plenty of dives left still to get to the 10 I booked both for me and for Andrea. Andrea passed the opportunity for these dives today, resting and defervescing from the tour-de-force of the day before. So at 8:20am I'm on the jetty again, ready to board for another adventure.

This time the dive master is again my favorite, Otto. He confides to me on the boat that has been diving daily for Club Med in the Maldives for the last 12 years straight! One can tell he knows this area like the back of his hands. He is confident but friendly, always smiling but secure, miniscule in weight but powerful.

The first dive today is at Nassimo. I go down to 21.4 meters, and stay down for a total of 47 minutes. I do it with Otto as my dive buddy. He has with him two small simple instruments to attract different types of fish. One is a metallic, thin, 6-inch long stick. He makes it vibrate in the water. This causes hundreds of 5-inch, bright blue fin trevally all converge on us. After a few minutes of vibrations, he and I are surrounded by what feels like thousands of these fish, in a large circle that engulfs us like a rainbow of sparking blue. It feels like the fish are celebrating us, dancing around us.

Later during the dive, he also sometimes rubs a plastic water bottle, which is supposed to attract bigger fish, such as turtles or rays, or even sharks. This time, he's less successful, but we are still immersed among thousands of fish, of at least a dozen different species all around us.

At some point, we spot three nurse sharks, at the bottom, under a coral reef, resting against the current. They look scary, as they are 2.5 meter (over 8 feet) long, but also calm, placid. Together with Otto, I get closer, only about a foot away from their mouth, right in front of them. They can be recognized not only for being so big, but also because they have two shark fins on top and also on the bottom of their bodies. I feel sad Andrea is not with me to see them.

While going from the first to the second scuba site, we see dolphins swimming near our boat while going. They look pretty dark, almost black, and jump up happily completely out of the water.

Interestingly, while the weather is warm and sunny, a gentle rain falls over us on the boat, and it feel unreal, given our clam and splendid surroundings, but there is a slightly darker cloud following us above.

The second dive is at the site called the Colosseum. I go down to 22 meters, for a total of 45 minutes. For both this morning dives, Otto has to let me breath for the last 5 minutes or so with his extra regulator, as I get quickly to less than 50 bars of air. I later realize this may be because I'm also getting sick, but certainly enjoy my times looking at more of this enchanted water world.

In the meanwhile, Andrea rests all morning in bed. Pietro and Paola relax in and around the pool, waiting for Andrea to wake up and me to get back.

In the afternoon, we spend more time in the pool, and then Andrea, Pietro and I also go to the gym. It is basically on the beach, with a beautiful view of the sea, and it is pleasant to play around with some of the machines and weights.

Andrea and Pietro then a play soccer match, one on one, on the sand. They go all out. They get to a tie of 5-5 in 'regulation' time, and a final score of 8-6after extra-time. They play under the rain, and come back drenched.

Later in the afternoon, around 5pm, we go to the beach volleyball court. Andrea, Pietro and I start playing volley ball. We soon attract a couple of other players. One is 'Raimondo,' who is probably a French

'Raymond' who pretends to know a word of two of Italian, and is short, about 50 years old, and friendly.

The other one is a Maldivian GO, Ajaz, dark, skinny with broad shoulders. He is about 5'11", which is super-tall for a Maldivian. Later, he tells us is story. He says he just started at Club Med, as a lifeguard. His last job was a steward on the taxi planes that hop from atoll to atoll. But he was too tall for the tiny cabin, and he felt that was not going to be a viable future for him.

He studies in his small southern atoll, and then for secondary school in Male. He says schools are good in the Maldives. For university, many of his countrymen and women go to India, Singapore, Australia, and other countries.

The teams for the beach volleyball game are Ajaz and Raimondo vs Andrea, Pietro and I. They won the first game, and we won the second game. It was a lot of fun, and I rejoiced seeing my sons becoming ever better players. Pietro even spiked a couple of times!

Wednesday, March 27

Every morning the sunrise is a bit different. I go and sit at the Iru bar, on the south-east side of the island, where there is the best view. The sun rises about 5 to 10 minutes after 6, but the time that one can spot the red circle changes every time, depending on the thickness of the clouds on the eastern horizon.

Yesterday, for example, it appeared early, as there where almost no clouds. Today there are a lot more clouds on the line of the horizon, even if the sky is mostly clear. I wait until after 6:30 to be able to see my beloved red giant. In five more minutes, the red giant transforms itself in a white bright light, which begins immediately to warm the skin.

Today I basically feel terrible all day long. My right ear hurts from diving. I feel basically half dead. I have a headache. It reminds me of the pain I had when I was a teenager and I would get frontal sinus inflammations. They were so debilitating that I would have to stay in bed sometimes for days. In fact, this is probably what has happened.

My physique, used to hours seated in comfortable air-conditioned surroundings in front of a computer, has not accepted the several hours of underwater life I've had in the last 48 hours or so. I feel my head if full of water, swollen, and any natural air pocket in my sinuses is full of mucus, which is slowly expanding given the inflammatory reaction.

I feel tired, strange, as in an out-of-body experience. There is no energy left in my muscles. I feel like my bones are broken down. My right heel still bothers me, a pre-Maldivian injury. My surroundings are unusual, the air ever warmer, deeply humid. I'm on the other side of my world, lost to my senses.

I seriously wander if I'll be able to dive again during this trip. This is particularly sad since Andrea is feeling much better, and would probably like to go diving today, but only if I also go. But I need to take a break. So we relax most of the day.

During our lunches and dinners, Suman is our waiter. He is Maldivian, dark, quiet, and super-nice. Each resort in the Maldives has to employ at 50%, or more, of its personnel from local people, by law.

He is clearly happy doing is job. He is caring, attentive to detail. His only wish is to see us smile. His only reward is to get a sincere 'thank you' from us. This is the secret of a rewarding life. One does not have to cure cancer or discover a new planet to make a difference in the world, or to feel important. Simple goals such as serving foreign tourists with attentiveness, respect, and outmost detailed care can be fulfilling.

At the bar by the pool, especially Pietro and I, but also Andrea and Paola, often fetch wonderful drinks, such as large iced tea, fresh orange juice, cocomango, strawberry daiquiri, mint tropical drink, and others. Pietro even gets by mistake a strawberry daiquiri with alcohol, but does not experience any drunken effects from it.

Andrea and Pietro play again beach soccer in the field with two small goals. Pietro in particular gets large scraping bleeding wounds in his knees, but is the least bothered by them, to Paola's dismay. The weather today is drizzling, albeit still conformably warm. We also play a wonderful game of bocce on the sand.

Thursday, March 28

I take another day off scuba to recover. I still do not feel well. When I walk barefooted on the hard and packed sand from our room to the swimming pool and bar, I feel the impact of my heels on the soil pounding like small bombs inside my head.

Andrea is feeling great. We go to the south-east side to snorkel a bit. Andrea and I venture to a small inhabited atoll just 40 yards off shore. Among many interesting things, we also spot a stingray in the shallow - less than a foot - waters. It's easily recognizable because of the characteristic shadow on the sea floor. Otherwise they can be hard to spot, as they are camouflaged, only slightly darker than the sand they swim on. They are cartilaginous fish, a bit like a flattened shark. They are sea bottom feeders, and are equipped with crushing teeth to grind the mollusks and crustaceans they sift out of the sand. A barbed spine on the top of the tail can deliver a very painful injury. This one must be a juvenile, as it is about 20 inches long. Mature rays can be up to 7 feet long.

Once in a while, we remind gently Pietro about his homework. And especially about the fact that he should try to read more. He does listen, and complies at times, even it is hard for him. He is a wonderful son.

Andrea, Pietro, and I, once again, spend long stretches of time playing water games of volleyball in the pool. These times are carefree, precious, joyous, priceless. All three of us enjoy this activity tremendously.

Andrea had remarked for the last couple of days that he had noticed only one good-looking girl in the village. She is tallish at about 5'7", white, slim, has light eyes, long hair, and wears a nice bikini. Andrea calls her 'la bonazza' ('the good-looking one,' in Italian slang). She seems to be always with a middle-aged woman who appears to be her mother.

I comment in my head, happily, that Andrea has perhaps for the first time spontaneously voiced his female interests. I'm sure he has had them for a while, but he is beginning to feel confident enough, sure enough of himself, and of me, to make his thoughts known.

Around 12 noon, there is water aerobics. I join, to exercise a bit and have fun. The moves are led by a friendly and energetic Indian GO, which his colleagues call 'United States of Punjab.' As the group gathers, I noticed that the 'bonazza' is also in the pool, and without her mother. So I move close to her.

From the pool's edge, Andrea is looking at my bold move. I try to get his attention, and signal for him to come and join water aerobics, as the opportunity to meet the girl he had been eyeing for a few days is right there for him to take. But he is not moving.

"Hello, where are you from?" were, I believe, the first words I uttered to the 'bonazza' as we moved together towards the water aerobics teacher. She looked at me in the friendliest of ways, with a shy but collaborative smile, and answered, "From Russia."

During water aerobics, we exchanged another ten phrases or so. She was gracious, affable, forthcoming. Her English was not fluent, but was good enough for a simple conversation. She was 14, her name was Anna, lived in Moscow, and was leaving a day after us. Close up, her eyes were of an unbelievable color, one I had never seen.

Once the 'ice' is broken, and the smile is returned, it's relatively easy to talk to women. In retrospect, we all had kind of noticed Anna and her mother had possibly also had an interest in us, and I had suspected Anna had become well aware of Andrea.

In the afternoon, at 2pm, all four of us go snorkeling again with the big group. I spot a clown trigger fish, with its characteristic large, round, white blotches. I point to it for Paola, who is delighted at the interesting sighting.

We also see, among herds of several fish, the unicorn. As the name implies, this fish has a unicorn jetting out of his face, in front of the eyes, for at least a couple of inches. Why, one wonders? I'm sure there is an evolutionary answer; I just do not know it.

Later, we go back and exercise in gym. We do some step master, abdominal exercises, biceps and triceps, deltoids, pectorals, and feel great afterwards.

We then play beach volley. We wait for Ajaz who is supposed to join us at 5pm, but he never comes. He tells us later he was too tired from doing lifeguard training all day. So the teams are Andrea and Pietro, against Paola and I. Paola actually reveals herself to be still quite a good team member, despite not having played in a while. I love the fact that she still shows a youthful side to the kids. Despite our best efforts, though, Andrea and Pietro win the set, deservingly.

Friday, March 29

This is the day I can finally resume diving. I'm finally smart enough to avoid eating too much for breakfast. I only have a tiny amount of cereals with some papaya and peaches. Very light food, so I won't burp anymore underwater.

The dive master for the morning dives is Martin. He must be at least 45 years old, has bright blond messy hair beaten by constantly being in ocean waters, has a constant smile, speaks and seems to me initially to be French. Later, while conversing with him, I find out he is originally from Vienna, Austria. He certainly has changed his life. I imagine how he would have been behind a desk in a cold office. I cannot even imagine him with a jacket and tie, it's impossible, given now his image is habitually that of a free ocean deep water diver.

The first of our dives this morning is at Coral Garden. In effect, we see some of the nicest corals so far. There are of a hundred different kinds and shapes. Their colors vary from orange, to white, to yellowish, to light purple. Andrea and I go down to a maximum depth of about 20 meters, and stay down a total of 49 minutes. Miraculously, or perhaps because my sinuses are indeed better, I do not run out of air!

The corals are indeed some of the most colorful and varied we ever see. Most are hermatypic corals, whose outer tissues are infused with zooxanthellae algae. These algae and the coral live in a symbiotic relationship, each dependent on the other. The algae photosynthesize from carbon dioxide and sunlight, to make food. The coral provides the algae with a safe home.

These zooxanthellae algae give the coral its color. So, is the algae die, the coral lose its color. That is why coral lost their color when the water was too hot, like in the 1998 coral bleaching episode, and why coral lose their color when taken out of the water.

For the second dive, we go back to Aquarium, which had been our very first open water dive and perhaps our favorite. We go to a depth of 19 meters, and stay down a total of 51 meters, which turns out to be the longest dive here in the Maldives. And I even had some air left, about 50 bars!

We rest after the two dives, not to repeat our previous mistake. I'm a bit worried to get sick again. In fact my mother had told me not to dive again. But I love it too much.

We spent time by the pool, and Anna the 14-year-old girl from Russia, and Andrea and Pietro familiarize with each other a bit more. We play volleyball in the pool. Anna is decent, and is age-appropriate shy but interested to interact with such new people, compared to her world in Moscow.

For the night dive, our appointment is at 5:45pm. Both Andrea and I were reluctant to do it until the end. But, after the two successful dives in the morning, and a plan for full rest in the afternoon, we are ready. I sense Andrea is particularly brave. First and foremost, he had said previously, including during this vacation, that he was too afraid to do a night dive. Secondly, he was just sick a couple of days previously, and that was caused by too much time in the water, which would be even worse this time. Thirdly, he knew I also had never done a night dive. I was particularly proud of his courage, and of his trusting of me and my judgment. He himself volunteered for the dive.

The dive master this time was again Martin. Trusted, calm, careful, friendly. The weather, instead, was probably the worst we ever had. It was raining. We even went by the scuba office at 5:15 to check if the dive was still on, but Otto and Emilie reassured us that 'Of course it was till on.'

Given the rain, we go just behind our own island, at a site called Disco Reef. As planned, Andrea and I hold hands during most of the dive. We end up going to a depth of 15 meters, and stay down in the total darkness for a total of about 45 minutes.

We see a lot of fish who are sleeping, remarkably. They just lay motionless on coral rocks. Parrot fish, big at 20 inches, fat, and colorful, are remarkable seen balanced on rock. One, once several torches illuminate him for a minute, finally wakes up and swims away, seeming annoyed.

Overall, the night dive is certainly interesting, in fact fascinating. It's amazing to see directly how much life and activities go one inside these waters, which from land or even a boat look black, dead, and even ominous. Below the surface, instead, all is alive, and peaceful. But we could not see as much as during a regular day dive, only what was in the narrow field of illumination.

Towards the end of the dive, now at only about 5 meter deep, we notice something remarkable and truly different. There is like a huge snow storm, in the water. Billions of tiny bits of white seem to be floating in the water, dancing around. Martin plays with a longer piece of white, like a tiny string of feather, with his metal thin stick. The fluff seems to be a tiny snake curling around and around his movements.

Once back on the ocean surface, if one turns the torch light in the water, this white snow storm can still be seen. Martin explains to us that this is plankton. The secret of these small worm-like tiny creatures is revealed. In fact, Andrea notices that they are attracted by our torch light.

Finally, after reading about it and studying it for years, I've seen plankton. Seeing how many billions and billions of them are just in one small part of the ocean, I understand how several bigger sea creatures, and even whales, can survive eating this. There is so much plankton in the ocean!

On the ocean surface, our lights also illuminate the rain coming down. It's quite a sight. Here too, billions and billions of tiny particles, which would be appreciated in day light, can be appreciated, as they are constantly coming down from above. It's a show that I could watch for hours.

I complete 8 dives, a miracle considering how I was feeling on Wednesday and Thursday. Andrea does a total of 6, which is really three times as much as he has ever done, and a great effort given his significant dehydration episode after the first three scuba dives. The only fish we had dreamed of seeing which we do not see are two. One is the whale shark, actually the largest fish in the world – up to 12 meters in length (remember, whales are not fish but mammals). We also missed manta rays.

We again try to stay up, but go to sleep before 9pm.

Saturday, March 30

This last full day on the island is probably the most relaxing. We are all now familiar with everything and everyone, we feel well, and we know how to best enjoy the fantastic opportunities at Club Med Kani, in the Maldives.

In the pool, Anna is laying around on one of the beach chairs with her mother. We get to know them better. Her mother, Yelena, is a lot more talkative than her daughter Anna. But her English is worst, so often Anna translates for her, as she is trying to recount their lives in Moscow.

It is clear they are a nice family. Her husband is working now, and her older son is busy in the university. They clearly have big plans for Anna, and are even looking at possible boarding schools in Switzerland. The mother I think has big dreams for her daughter.

Daughter and mother have the same eyes. The color is indescribable, amazing. It's a light grey with bluish and faintly green accents. I've never seen anything even similar. I think that they must have some Siberian ancestry, as they remind of something cold and vast, foreign and unknown.

While we play more volleyball in the pool, I start counting our touiches in different languages. English. Italian. Spanish. French. Then I ask Anna to count in Russian. She happily complies.

'Raz, dva, tri, chitiri,' is what we hear she says when counting from one to four. We like the 'four' in particular, as she accents both the first and third syllable. Google says that one, two, three, four, in Russian are 'odin, dva, tri, chetyre.' We were pretty close, except for the 'one.' I wonder if 'raz' is 'one' in Moscow's dialect.

In the afternoon, we return to snorkel in south-east side of island. Anna and Yelena accompany us. Paola and Pietro are busy looking at the many fish present in the crystal clear shallow water. Andrea and I are busier entertaining a simple with Anna and her mother while also pretending to snorkel. Andrea remembers also seeing porcupine fish, characteristic for their sharp spines on the body. We also spot a parrot fish, and a lion fish.

At 4:30pm, we get to the jetty, where our fast boat awaits with our ready luggage, to take us, after eight wonderful days, back to Male, and to the airport.

Anna and Yelena come to say good bye. Yelena takes a picture of Andrea and Anna together. They are all smiles. While we wait in the boat about 10 minutes before taking off, both of them wait patiently on the dock, looking at us. As the boat speeds away from the jetty, both Anna and Yelena wave their arms even more widely. They were nice.

Sunday, March 31

Doha, the capital of Qatar, is an amazing city. There are hundreds of modern, sparkling, futuristically-shaped skyscrapers. The plane from Male to Doha leaves the gate 15 minutes ahead of time, and we end up in Doha, after a pleasant flight, at least half an hour early. There are dozens of cranes all over town, mostly seemingly aimed at building more irregularly-shaped and tall buildings.

You can see the future is here. There are more cranes than in any city I've ever seen. Even more than in Kuala Lumpur, the capital of Malaysia, which was the last city which impressed me for the numbers of new constructions of skyscrapers going up at the same time.

The last flight back, Doha-New York, is about 14 hours long. This is when a lot of the travel diary was written. I'm mesmerized by the large computer display showing our flight progress. We go from the Arabian Peninsula, to the Gulf of Mexico, over to Turkey, the Mediterranean, then the Balkans, mid-Europe, and finally the vast Atlantic. We fly at high speed over so many cultures, so much history. The world is indeed getting smaller, when two continents usually so vastly separated not only by distance but even more by culture can be jumped to and from so easily.

I ask Andrea what was the thing he liked the most about this trip. To my amazement, and joy, he says, "The fact that we four were together 24/7 for 9 days straight." I could not have wished for a better answer.

Acknowledgements

Andrea Berghella
Paola Luzi

www.ingramcontent.com/pod-product-compliance
Lightning Source LLC
Chambersburg PA
CBHW030304030426
42337CB00012B/585